Workbook for You're Leading Now!

A Six-Step Strategy for Building and Leading Dynamic Teams

by Tiffany Timmons-Saab

Illustrated by Amy Koch Johnson

Here are the steps as a reference to use.
It's a quick glance at the six-steps you should do.

Step 4 = Measure Results

Step 3 - Play the Game/Execute

Step 2 = Buy-In Commitment

Step 5 = Debrief/ Evaluate Effectiveness

Step 1 = Vision, Goals, and Planning

Step 6 = Constructive Feedback and Appropriate Consequences

The Six-Step Path to Lead and Succeed Workbook

> If you like your results,
> Keep doing as you do.
> If you want to improve,
> Let's first start with you!

Congratulations! You are a LEADER.
You get to coach, lead, and mentor your team to success.

Will it be easy to do? _____

Has it been easy? _____

When you first took on the leadership role,
what did you expect to happen?

Have events held up to your expectations?

If not, what has been different?

What do you wish you knew now that you didn't know then?

Is leadership important to you? Why?

"No team can out perform the limitations of its leader. If you want your team to get better, you have to get better."
(Hanson + Hanson, 2007)

What's Your Why?

Do you believe it is worthwhile to get better?

What are your strengths as a leader?

In what areas could you grow as a leader?

FOCUS

"Hope is not a strategy" – it is a key factor in the right mindset.

Why is hope important?

Mindset

What does mindset mean?

"Men and women are limited not by the place of their birth, not by the color of their skin, but the size of their hope."

(John Johnson)

"Hope is the foundational quality of change." (Alfred Adler)

What's the difference between "Hope" as a strategy and "Hope" as a part of your mindset?

NOTES TO SELF-

"Discipline is the necessary ingredient that separates 'the dreamer' from 'the doer.'" (Ed Rehkopf

True or False

T or F – There is something you can do every day to change your circumstances.

T or F – It's not what happens to you, it's how you handle it.

T or F – Failure is an event, not a person.

T or F – Cultivating the right mindset requires daily attention.

T or F – Blaming and excuses are not part of a good mindset.

T or F – Taking 100% responsibility for your life is a positive mindset.

T or F – Hope is a good strategy.

Creating Accountability is critical to your success as a leader. What is accountability?

Does your team hold itself accountable?

How?

How should accountability optimally look for your team?

What are the 3D's to make your plan work:

D:

D:

D:

**In reviewing the 6 steps,
which ones are you most confident you do well?**

"To win in
the marketplace
you must first
win in the
workplace."
(Doug Conant)

**What do you think
your team would say?**

Which steps could you benefit from improving on?

"Managers help people see themselves as they are; Leaders help people to see themselves better than they are." (Jim Rohn)

Reflection

What makes you think this?

What if you don't see progress?

Qualify

It can be uncomfortable to grow, because it means change, and changing is difficult. Ironically, isn't that what you ask your team to do every day in order to get better?

Are you open to change in order to grow? YES or NO

What 3 ways do you specifically want to grow?

"The answer to the question 'when do I start?' is NOW." (John Maxwell)

Action

Step 1: Vision, Goals, and Planning

True or False

T or F – I always start with a vision for each project my team takes on.

T or F – I share this vision clearly with the team.

T or F – We use this vision to stay focused on our mission to make daily decisions.

T or F – As a leader, it is my responsibility to understand each team member so I can communication with them accordingly.

Do your answers help or hurt you and your team?

Why is a vision so important?

77% of senior managers want to raise their level of employee engagement, but only 41% of them communicate personally with employees about plans and goals on a regular basis." (Elizabeth, 2014)

Do you think each member of your team shares your vision?

What are the implications if they don't?

What role does a vision, and your goals play in your decision making?

 Plus include your team's vision and goals on a daily basis?

"If you think it takes time to be clear up front, it's nothing compared to the time miscommunication takes." (Hanson & Hanson 2007)

<u>What are standards?</u>

<u>How can you use expectations to set standards?</u>

YES or NO

When you work through goals; are they SMART?

Specific Y or N
Measurable Y or N
Achievable (with a stretch) Y or N
Reasonable Y or N
Timely Y or N

"In preparing for battle I have always found that plans are useless, but planning is indispensable."

(Eisenhower)

"You've got to think about big things while you're doing small things, so that all the small things go in the right direction." (Alvin Toffler)

Communication can get fuzzy, so how can you ensure each team member is crystal clear on "their part"?

Responsibility

"People are creatures of emotion and reason. The best performers want to belong to an organization that's on a mission, and they need to see how they're contributing to that mission."

(Harpst, 2008)

"Goals. There's no telling what you can do when you get inspired by them. There's no telling what you can do when you believe in them. There's no telling what will happen when you act upon them." (Jim Rohn)

Notes-

UNDERSTANDING OTHERS

How important is it to
understand others
when communicating?

As the leader, it is your responsibility to understand each team member and communicate in their language, because each person is unique. The Behavioral Model focuses 100% on HOW people communicate. It's not a measure of intelligence, skills, experience, or education.

The Behavioral Model is HOW WE ACT, it's our behavior. Research has consistently shown there are 4 styles that emerge. There are resources to take assessments that summarize styles for yourself and others. While these can be very helpful, I encourage you to hone your observation skills and read others in the moment, a tool that will build your communication style for anyone, anywhere.

There are 4 basic styles of communication (each person will be a mix, and as you become better at understanding others, you will quickly see the dominant 1 or 2, possibly 3 styles each person has).

"Communication is a skill that you can learn. It's like riding a bicycle or typing. If you're willing to work at it, you can rapidly improve the quality of every part of your life."

(Brian Tracy)

"All people exhibit all four behavioral factors in varying degrees of intensity."

(W.M. Marston)

When you understand what they need, you will speak their language and communicate more deeply and effectively.

On the UNDERSTANDING OTHERS chart you will learn about the 4 styles and how to recognize them and the behaviors and characteristics you will observe.

The more you truly focus on the other person, the words they use, their pace, and how they communicate, their dominant styles will quickly become obvious.

Although William M. Marston is credited with creating the DISC model, its roots actually go back to 444 B.C.!

"If you want to change others, you must first change yourself."
(Judy Suiter)

The first step is observing their pace - are they faster-paced or more cautious sharing their thoughts and through their actions. Then, as you listen to their words, what is most important to them?

Do they focus on the task, the goal, and the process, or do they zero in on people and team?

The second chart, How to Coach Each Style, gives you the Dos and Don'ts of situational communication. You will probably have lightbulbs go off as you start to recognize people in your life and how you can be a better communicator with each person.

"Communication is everything."

(Lee Lacocca)

"The most important thing in communication is hearing what isn't said." (Peter Drucker)

Take lots of notes, think of those you know, and they ways you can become better at understanding and motivating others.

Understanding Others
What do you observe?

Fast-Paced

Meet the D
The Dominant

D - Could come across as intimidating and impatient.

Decisive
Direct
Competitive
Favorite word is GO
Self-starter
Driver
Likes challenges
Fast-paced
Always in a hurry
Quick decision makers
Risk taker
Results focused
Strong-willed
Asks "what"
Bold movements and Loud vocal tones
Lack of actions causes stress to the "D"

Meet the I
The Inspiring

I - Could come across as unorganized, impulsive or fake.

Influencing
Impressive
Persuasive
Charming
Extrovert
Encourager
Optimist
Story tellers
Lots of voice inflection
Asks "who"
Big body movement when talking
Social
People and relationship focused
Personable
High Energy
Rejection causes stress to the "I"

Task Oriented

People Oriented

Meet the C
The Calculating

C - Could come across as unemotional, cold and overly critical.

Cautious
Objective
Analytical
Systematic
Perfectionist
Attention to detail
Skeptical
Standard setters
Likes proof
Follows the rules
Organized
Conscientious
High standards
Distrusting
Asks "why" and "how"
Inconsistency causes stress to the "C"

Meet the S
The Supportive

S - Could come across as procrastinators or withdrawn.

Steady
Team player
Supportive
Loyal
Amiable
Shows patience
Relaxed pace, not in a hurry
Uncomfortable with change
Like the predictable
Good listener
Finishes tasks
Dependable
Non-confrontational
Shuts down in arguments
Conflict causes stress to the "S"

Cautious

Adapted from W.M. Marston's DISC Model (Bonnstetter & Widrick, 2001; Straw, 2002; Wiley & Sons, 2013)

How to Work With Each Style
Do's and Don'ts

Fast-Paced

Working With the D

Do be direct and get to the point
Do persuade with desired results
Do focus on bottom line
Do support
Do provide big goals
Do outline boundaries
Do confront disagreements face-to-face
Do give deadlines, then autonomy

Don't be slow, beat around the bush, unsure, waste their time, or tell stories.

Working With the I

Do show enthusiasm, smile
Do put details in writing
Do offer structure -helps them focus on priorities
Do work with on time management
Do ask for their opinion
Do get to action items
Do encourage team work
Do talk personal, but not too much
Do focus on the FUN and PEOPLE part

Don't dismiss their ideas, be impersonal, or embarrass.

Task Oriented

People Oriented

Working With the C

Do be exact
Do prepare in advance
Do support ideas with logic and facts to build credibility for both sides
Do give time to think.
Do use facts and explain tasks logically
Do what you say you will do
Do be direct and focus on process and detail
 Do check in only when necessary with predetermined deadlines
Do slow down your pace if you are a D or I
Do be objective with feedback

Don't go too fast, be informal, or too personal.

Working With the S

Do be sincere
Do break the ice with a friendly approach
Do give them time to think about issue with a deadline
Do give them space to think and answer
Do allow for silence
Do recognize the job well done
Do be patient and kind
Do caution them to not over commit
Do create a nonthreatening environment
Do give them time to adjust to change
Do offer reassurance

Don't rush them, interrupt, or dismiss their concerns about change.

Cautious

Adapted from W.M. Marston's DISC Model (Bonnstetter & Widrick, 2001; Straw, 2002; Wiley & Sons, 2013)

How would you define your personal communication style?

Do you see where your team members would fit?

Which style do you get along with easily?

> "You can get everything in life you want, if you help people get what they want."
>
> (Zig Ziglar)

Which style is a struggle for you to interact with?

17

Step 2: Getting the Commitment

How do you get commitment and engagement from your team?

Are you familiar with WIIFM? What does it stand for?

The important piece of gaining commitment is not telling others what they should do. It's a deeper level of communication and understanding to make sure you are working toward a common goal together. Listen and ask questions of your team.

NOTES-

How can you do something different to improve those relationships that are more challenging?

"84% of employees in the U.S. claim their relationship with their boss is the top determining factor for whether they try to move up in the company—or find work elsewhere."
(National Business Research Institute)

What are 3 actions you can take to improve communication and understanding of your vision to your team?

Action

Use the 'Understanding Others' chart to create relevant questions; questions that will connect with each team member so they can answer WIIFM. What are some questions you can use?

"There is only one rule for being a good talker learn to listen."

(Christopher Morley)

"If this stat doesn't convince you to explore solutions to your employee engagement problem, nothing will: companies with engaged employees outperform those without by up to 202%. That is not a typo."
(Dale Carnegie)

T. O. L. I. S. T. E. N.
is all about action, it means-

T.

O.

L.

I.

S.

T.

E.

N.

How do these principles play into your leadership?

N.

I.

C.

E.

F.

E.

A.

R.

Don't be afraid to shift strategy with the input of your team; showing you listen and use their input will yield bigger results than you "being right."

Are you reluctant (even a little) to use your team's ideas and input?

If so, why?

How can you use the team's ideas to improve the overall direction?

Are you sure you have each team member's commitment?   Y or N

Are you positive? Y or N

If YES, then let's move on...

What are 3 actions you can take
to get commitment from your team?

"Connect the dots between
individual roles and the goals
of the organization. When people
see that connection, they get a lot
of energy out of work. They feel the
importance, dignity, and
meaning in their job."
(Blanchard & Blanchard, 2012)

STEP 3: Execute the Plan; Run the Race

Ever heard the term "failing forward"?

It's difficult to let your employees fail, especially when you can jump in and make it right for them.

Have you done this in the past?

Did you get the results you wanted?

Why or why not?

> "Complaining = Negativity, and Negativity costs the U.S. Economy between $250 to $300 billion every year in lost productivity."
> (Gordon, 2008)

How did a leader let you fail in the past?

What did you learn?

How can you let your employees fail?

Are you willing to do that?

If not, how does it impact you or the team?

Do you feel like complaining affects your team?

"90% of doctor visits are stress related, according to Centers of Disease Control and Prevention, and the #1 cause of office stress is coworkers and their complaining."
(Gordon, 2008)

How will you create a culture of no complaining?

Do you have a culture of no excuses?

How will you create a culture of no excuses?

What are 3 action steps you can take to help your team run the race?

"Praise only works with three types of people: men, women, and children."

Action

NOTES-

Step 4: Keeping Score

"Numbers create accountability, accountable people appreciate numbers, numbers create clarity, commitment, and teamwork. You can solve problems faster." (Wickman, 2012)

"What gets measured gets done, what gets measured and fed back gets done well, what gets rewarded gets repeated." (John E. Jones)

Keeping score isn't only about winning, it's about measuring your growth and progress.

On a Scale of 1 – 10, with 10 being the best, how well do you track measurable results that help employees focus on the right behaviors?

Do you think tracking measurables makes a difference?

If yes, how so?

If you are not yet a 10, how can you become a 10?

"Inspect what you expect." (Zig Ziglar)

Sometimes I focus too much on what hasn't been achieved yet, instead of recognizing what has been accomplished and allowing that progress to motivate me and the team.

T   or   F

How do you celebrate the progress your team makes?

What can you do differently to recognize progress that has been achieved?

◆◆◆◆◆◆◆◆◆◆◆   ◆◆◆◆◆◆◆◆◆◆◆◆

List 3 things you could start measuring immediately:

What is a KPI? A Key Performance Indicator creates a measurable that supports the goal. You will also see this in a company scorecard. According to Gino Wickman, author of Traction, every person in an organization owns a number.

"In the business world, measurement accelerates learning and stimulates innovation. Clear measures help people move toward a goal, giving them tangible feedback on their innovation and effort." (Harpst, 2008)

Brainstorming-

Step 5: Debriefing

Debriefing is all about evaluation; evaluating what worked, what didn't work, and what the team needs to do to improve next time.

Do you always include the whole team
(at least those who were involved with the project)?   Y or N

How can you eliminate excuses and blaming others?

As a team, we identify clearly what the problem is and come
to an agreement on the problem before we jump to a solution.
T or F

Debriefing is easy to skip because you move on to the next urgent item.
If you skip this step, what are you communicating to the team?

On a scale of 1-10 (10 being the highest), I recognize good work and
encourage my team to recognize good work they see in others.

⇨ ⇨ ⇨ ⇨ ⇨ ⇨ ⇨ ⇨ ⇨ ⇨ ⇨ ⇨ ⇨ ⇨ ⇨ ⇨ ⇨ ⇨ ⇨ ⇨

What would your team say about your answer?

How do you recognize achievement on your team?

Do your team members feel comfortable recognizing others?

"The number-one reason most Americans leave their jobs is that they don't feel appreciated. In fact, 65% of people surveyed said they got no recognition for good work last year."
(Clifton & Rath, 2004)

"60% of Best-in-Class organizations stated that employee recognition is extremely valuable in driving individual performance."
(Laurano, 2013)

How do you solicit feedback from your team?

How do you incorporate your team's feedback to find solutions?

Feedback

What are 3 action steps you can take to consistently engage your team's feedback?

"Praise and commendation from managers was rated the top motivator for performance, beating out other noncash and financial incentives, by a majority of workers."
(67%)
(McKinsey, 2009)

Action

Step 6: Follow Up: Constructive Feedback and Appropriate Consequences

"Too many negative interactions compared to positive interactions at work can decrease productivity of a team, according to Barbara Fredrickson's research at the University of Michigan." (Gordon, 2008)

True or False

I am overly critical of my team's failures and feel defeated at time?
T or F

I am comfortable giving constructive feedback and I see progress from my team as a result. T or F

Even if I get busy, I will follow up with team members to give constructive feedback or appropriate consequences with a solution-minded focus? T or F

What would your team say about your Follow Up?

"Appreciate everything your associates do for the business. Nothing else can quite substitute for a few well-chosen, well-timed, sincere words of praise. They're absolutely free and worth a fortune."
(Sam Walton)

Is it consistent?

Is it actionable?

"Positivity only works when it is sincere and honest."
(Blanchard, 2002)

"Praise progress, it's a moving target."
(Blanchard, 2002)

31

Follow Up is the time to coach the team through areas that need improvement. Think of it like this: The Debrief is the locker room meeting after the game, and the Follow Up is the time to focus on improvement. The Follow Up is the time to review progress, balance what's been accomplished with what remains ahead. It is also a time for appropriate consequences. This isn't negative as some will believe. Your follow up, as the leader, shows your commitment to the team and their personal growth. This action of personal attention speaks louder than any words possibly could.

Have any members of my team been hurt because of my lack of follow up?

How has this affected my team?

> "Ninety-nine percent of all failures come from people who have a habit of making excuses."
> (George W. Carver)

How can I get better at follow up?

Consequences are

- Determined in advance (or established after a failure and used for any reoccurrence)
- Mutually understood
- Timely
- Consistent"
(Brandyworks.com)

> "Criticize the performance if the performance deserves criticism, but remember to praise the performer. Criticize in private, praise in public."
>
> (Zig Ziglar)

> "It is the front-line staff who best know what needs to be fixed and how to do it."
> (Quint Studer)

Consequences are not

- Angry or reactive
- Surprises
- Unreasonable or out of proportion

How will this make a difference for my team?

What are 3 action items you can take to follow up with your team?

Notes-

Action

"Leadership is not so much about what you do. It's about what you can inspire, encourage, empower, and coach others to do."

(Gordon, 2010)

Brainstorm-

"The challenge of leadership is to be strong, but not rude; be kind, but not weak; be bold, but not bully; be thoughtful, but not lazy; be humble, but not timid; be proud, but not arrogant; have humor, but without folly."

(Jim Rohn)

Conclusion:

You make hundreds of choices each day, are you ready to make the choice to start this circle and start over and over and over again?

Do you still think it is worth the effort to learn and grow to become a better leader and hold your team accountable?

Why?

What's In It For You?

"Enterprises that engage in a formal program of coaching experience significant benefits, ranging from improved morale and engagement from people who recognize their employer's commitment to their development, to enhanced performance resulting from a focus on the fundamentals of the business, and to pride in belonging to a high performing operation."
(Ed Rehkopf)

"Teams are the primary unit of performance for increasing numbers [profits] in organizations."
(Katzenbach & Smith, 1992)

"Leaders never outgrow the need to change."
(John Maxwell)

Let's wrap this up with the <u>Could Do, Want To and Will Do</u> exercise;
(This is a great one to do with your team as well!):

Mindset   Results   Planning   Coaching

What are 12 things you COULD DO in the next 90 days?

What are 8 things you WANT TO DO in the next 90 days?

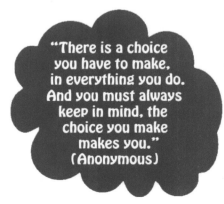

"There is a choice
you have to make,
in everything you do.
And you must always
keep in mind, the
choice you make
makes you."
(Anonymous)

What are 4 things you WILL DO in the next 90 days?
(For a sample 90 Day Plan, visit our website).
A 90 Day Plan gives you focus with specific action items and deadlines.
Each person on your team should always be working within a 90 Day Plan.

What can you do to increase your chances of success?

Last question – do you need accountability on this?

References

Blanchard, K. H., Ballard, J., Thompkins, C., & Lacinak, T. (2002). Whale Done!: The Power of Positive Relationships. New York: Simon & Schuster Adult Publishing Group.

Blanchard, K., & Blanchard, S. (2012). Do your people really know what you expect from them? Fast Company. From https://www.fastcompany.com/1767714/do-your-people-really-know-what-you-expect-them

Bonnstetter, B.J., Suiter, J.I., Widrick, R.J. (2001), The Universal Language DiSC, A Reference Manual. Target Training International.

Burley-Allen, M. (2007). Listening: The Forgotten Skill: A Self-teaching Guide. New York: Coach Series.

Clifton, D. O., & Rath, T. (2004). How Full is your Bucket? [Positive Strategies for Work and Life]. New York: Simon & Schuster Audio.

Elizabeth. (2014). Why employee voice results in employee engagement #infographic. Employee Engagement, http://www.thesocialworkplace.com/2014/02/why-employee-voice-results-in-employee-engagement-infographic/

Wickman, G. (2012). Traction: Get a Grip on Your Business. BenBella Books.

Gordon, J. (2008). The No Complaining Rule: Positive Ways to Deal with Negativity at Work. Chichester, United Kingdom: Wiley, John & Sons.

Gordon, J. (2010). Soup: A Recipe to Nourish your Team and Culture. Chichester, United Kingdom: Wiley, John & Sons.

Hanson, T., & Hanson, B. Z. (2007). Who Will Do What by When? How to Improve Performance, accountability and trust with integrity. Wayne, PA: Power Publications, Inc.

Harpst, G. (2008). Six Disciplines Execution Revolution: Solving the one Business Problem that Makes Solving all Other Problems Easier. New York, NY: Six Disciplines Publishing.

John Wiley & Sons, Inc. (2013). Everything DiSC Management Interaction Guide

Katzenbach, J. R., & Smith, D. K. (1992). The Wisdom of Teams: Creating the High-Performance Organization. Boston, MA: Harvard Business School Press.

Laurano, M. (2013). The Power of Employee Recognition. Retrieved from http://go.globoforce.com/rs/globoforce/images/AberdeenReportNovember2013.pdf

McKinsey. (2009). Motivating People: Getting Beyond Money. From http://www.mckinsey.com/business-functions/organization/our-insights/motivating-people-getting-beyond-money

Miller, B. C. (2006). Keeping Employees Accountable for Results: Quick Tips for Busy Managers. New York, NY: AMACOM.

Pici, J. and Pici, D. (2008). Sell Naked On the Phone, Stripping Away the Barriers to Your Success in Sales. Personality Insights: Atlanta, GA.

Straw, J. (2002). The 4-Dimensional Manager, DiSC Strategies for Managing Different People in the Best Ways. Berrett-Koehler Publishers, Inc.: San Francisco, CA.

Stoltzfus T. (2008) Coaching Questions, A Coach's Guide to Powerful Asking Skills. Tony Stoltzfus, Virgina Beach, VA.

Additional Resources:

Journal of Leadership Studies

National Business Research Institute

Want more?

Order the workbook for You're Leading Now!

Learn more about our training and coaching programs for sales, leadership, presentation skills, and recruiting customization.

Schedule a complimentary session to find out if our programs would work for you.

www.tiffanytimmons.com

The Timmons Group is a leading business transformation firm, energizing growth through cultural change and building human value. Well known for the ability to anticipate, interpret, and facilitate personal and professional growth, the Timmons Group utilizes their proprietary VMT (Variable Mindset Training) and Practice Teams to deliver tangible results.

About the Author

Tiffany Timmons-Saab
Founder
The Timmons Group

With a strong ability to customize and integrate her expertise into various industries, Tiffany has delivered professional coaching, training, and recruiting services to local, regional, and national companies.

As a published author, speaker, and consultant, Tiffany creates training and coaching programs that allow her to adjust messages in real time based on audience participation. Her expressive style has helped business owners focus on results while building human value in their organizations.

She is Ziglar Performance Group and ActionCoach certified. She also holds a Bachelor of Business Administration from the University of Kentucky and a Master of Business Administration.

She currently lives in Scottsdale, Arizona, with her husband and three children.

Workbook ISBN# 978-0-9995556-5-1

Ideas + Actions = Results

Ideas + Actions = Results

Ideas + Actions = Results

Ideas + Actions = Results

Ideas + Actions = Results

Ideas + Actions = Results

Ideas + Actions = Results

Ideas + Actions = Results

Ideas + Actions = Results

Ideas + Actions = Results

CPSIA information can be obtained
at www.ICGtesting.com
Printed in the USA
BVHW021847240920
589570BV00012B/819